POPE FRANCIS

Antiquum ministerium

Apostolic Letter
Issued "Motu Proprio"
Instituting
the Ministry of Catechist

Cover Image:
© Charlotta Smeds

00120 Città del Vaticano
Tel. 06.698.45780
E-mail: commerciale.lev@spc.va

ISBN 978-88-266-0629-3

www.vatican.va

www.libreriaeditricevaticana.va

1. The ministry of Catechist in the Church is an ancient one. Theologians commonly hold that the first examples are already present in the writings of the New Testament. The service of catechesis may be traced back to those "teachers" mentioned by the Apostle in writing to the community of Corinth: "Some people God has designated in the Church to be, first, apostles; second, prophets; third, teachers; then, mighty deeds; then, gifts of healing, assistance, administration, and varieties of tongues. Are all apostles? Are all prophets? Are all teachers? Do all work mighty deeds? Do all have gifts of healing? Do all speak in tongues? Do all interpret? Strive eagerly for the greatest spiritual gifts. But I shall show you a still more excellent way" (*1 Cor* 12:28-31).

Saint Luke begins his Gospel by stating: "I too have decided, after investigating everything accurately anew, to write it down in an orderly sequence for you, most excellent Theophilus, so that you may realize the certainty of the teachings you have received" (*Lk* 1:3-4). The evangelist seems to be well aware that his writings offer a specific form of instruction that can give firm assurance to those already baptized. The Apostle Paul, for his part, tells the Galatians that: "one who is being instructed in the word should share all good things with his instructor" (*Gal* 6:6). As is evident, this text provides yet another detail; it speaks of the communion of life as a sign of the fruitfulness of an authentic catechesis.

2. From the beginning, the Christian community was characterized by many different forms of ministry carried out by men and women who, obedient to the working of the Holy Spirit, devoted their lives to the building up of the Church. At times, the charisms that the Spirit constantly pours out on the baptized took on a visible and tangible form of immediate service to the Christian community, one recognized as an indispensable *diakonia* for the community. The Apostle Paul authoritatively attests to this when he states that "there are different kinds of spiritual gifts but the same Spirit; there

are different forms of service but the same Lord; there are different workings but the same God who produces all of them in everyone. To each individual the manifestation of the Spirit is given for some benefit. To one is given through the Spirit the expression of wisdom; to another the expression of knowledge according to the same Spirit; to another faith by the same Spirit; to another gifts of healing by the one Spirit; to another mighty deeds; to another prophecy; to another discernment of spirits; to another varieties of tongues; to another interpretation of tongues. But one and the same Spirit produces all of these, distributing them individually to each person as he wishes" (*1 Cor* 12:4-11).

Within the broader charismatic tradition of the New Testament, then, we can see that certain baptized persons exercised the ministry of transmitting in a more organic and stable form related to different situations in life the teaching of the apostles and evangelists (cf. SECOND VATICAN ECUMENICAL COUNCIL, Dogmatic Constitution on Divine Revelation *Dei Verbum*, 8). The Church wished to acknowledge this service as a concrete expression of a personal charism that contributed greatly to the exercise of her mission of evangelization. This glance at the life of the first Christian communities engaged in the spread of the Gospel also encourages the Church in our day to appreciate possible new ways for her to remain faithful to the word of the Lord so that his Gospel can be preached to every creature.

3. The history of evangelization over the past two millennia clearly shows the effectiveness of the mission of catechists. Bishops, priests and deacons, together with many men and women in the consecrated life, devoted their lives to catechetical instruction so that the faith might be an effective support for the life of every human being. Some of them also gathered around themselves others of their brothers and sisters sharing the same charism, and founded religious orders wholly dedicated to catechesis.

Nor can we forget the countless lay men and women who directly took part in the spread of the Gospel through catechetical instruction. Men and women of deep faith, authentic witnesses of holiness, who in some cases were also founders of Churches and eventually died as martyrs. In our own day too, many competent and dedicated catechists are community leaders in various parts of the world and carry out a mission invaluable for the transmission and growth of the faith. The long line of blesseds, saints and martyrs who were catechists has significantly advanced the Church's mission and deserves to be recognized, for it represents a rich resource not only for catechesis but also for the entire history of Christian spirituality.

4. Beginning with the Second Vatican Ecumenical Council, the Church has come to a renewed appreciation of the importance of lay involvement in the work of evangelization. The Council Fathers repeatedly emphasized the great need for the lay faithful to be engaged directly, in the various ways their charism can be expressed, in the "*plantatio Ecclesiae*" and the development of the Christian community. "Worthy of praise too is that army of catechists, both men and women, to whom missionary work among the nations is so indebted, who imbued with an apostolic spirit make an outstanding and absolutely necessary contribution to the spread of the faith and the Church by their great work. In our days, when there are so few clerics to evangelize such great multitudes and to carry out the pastoral ministry, the role of catechists is of the

highest importance" (cf. SECOND VATICAN ECUMENICAL COUNCIL, Decree on the Church's Missionary Activity *Ad Gentes*, 17).

Along with the important teaching of the Council, mention should be made of the constant interest of the Popes, the Synod of Bishops, the Episcopal Conferences and individual Bishops who, in recent decades have contributed to a significant renewal of catechesis. The *Catechism of the Catholic Church*, the Apostolic Exhortation *Catechesi Tradendae*, the *General Catechetical Directory*, the *General Directory for Catechesis* and the recent *Directory for Catechesis*, as well as the many national, regional and diocesan Catechisms, have confirmed the centrality of a catechesis that gives priority to the education and ongoing formation of believers.

5. Without prejudice to the Bishop's mission as the primary catechist in his Diocese, one which he shares with his presbyterate, or to the particular responsibility of parents for the Christian formation of their children (cf. CIC can. 774 §2; CCEO can. 618), recognition should be given to those lay men and women who feel called by virtue of their baptism to cooperate in the work of catechesis (cf. CIC

can. 225; CCEO cans. 401 and 406). This presence is all the more urgently needed today as a result of our increasing awareness of the need for evangelization in the contemporary world (cf. Apostolic Exhortation *Evangelii Gaudium*, 163-168), and the rise of a globalized culture (cf. Encyclical Letter *Fratelli Tutti*, 100, 138). This requires genuine interaction with young people, to say nothing of the need for creative methodologies and resources capable of adapting the proclamation of the Gospel to the missionary transformation that the Church has undertaken. Fidelity to the past and responsibility for the present are necessary conditions for the Church to carry out her mission in the world.

Awakening personal enthusiasm on the part of all the baptized and reviving the awareness of their call to carry out a proper mission in the community demands attentiveness to the voice of the Spirit, who is unfailingly present and fruitful (cf. CIC can. 774 §1; CCEO can. 617). Today, too, the Spirit is calling men and women to set out and encounter all those who are waiting to discover the beauty, goodness, and truth of the Christian faith. It is the task of pastors to support them in this process and to enrich the life of the Christian community through the recognition of lay ministries capable of contributing to the transformation of society through the "penetration of Christian values into the social, political and economic sectors" (*Evangelii Gaudium*, 102).

6. The lay apostolate is unquestionably "secular". It requires that the laity "seek the kingdom of God by engaging in temporal affairs and directing them according to God's will" (cf. SECOND VATICAN ECUMENICAL COUNCIL Dogmatic Constitution on the Church *Lumen Gentium*, 31). In their daily life, interwoven with family and social relationships, the laity come to realize that they "are given this special vocation: to make the Church present and fruitful in those places and circumstances where it is only through them that she can become the salt of the earth" (ibid., 33). We do well to remember, however, that in addition to this apostolate, "the laity can be called in different ways to more immediate cooperation in the apostolate of the hierarchy, like those men and women who helped the apostle Paul in the Gospel, working hard in the Lord" (ibid.).

The role played by catechists is one specific form of service among others within the Christian community. Catechists are called first to be expert in the pastoral service of transmitting the faith as it develops through its different stages from the initial proclamation of the *kerygma* to the instruction that presents our new life in Christ and prepares for the sacraments of Christian initiation, and then to the ongoing formation that can allow each person to give an accounting of the hope within them (cf. *1 Pet* 3:15). At the same time, every catechist must be a witness to the faith, a teacher and mystagogue, a companion and pedagogue, who teaches for the Church. Only through prayer, study, and direct participation in the life of the community can they grow in this identity and the integrity and responsibility that it entails (cf. PONTIFICAL COUNCIL FOR THE PROMOTION OF THE NEW EVANGELIZATION, *Directory for Catechesis*, 113).

7. With great foresight, Saint Paul VI issued the Apostolic Letter *Ministeria Quaedam* with the intention not only of adapting the ministries of Lector and Acolyte to changed historical circumstances (cf. Apostolic Letter *Spiritus Domini*), but also of encouraging Episcopal Conferences to promote other ministries, including that of Catechist. "In addi-

tion to the ministries common to the entire Latin Church, nothing prevents Episcopal Conferences from asking the Apostolic See for the institution of others, which for particular reasons, they consider necessary or very useful in their own region. Among these are, for example, the offices of *Porter*, *Exorcist* and *Catechist*". The same pressing invitation is found in the Apostolic Exhortation *Evangelii Nuntiandi*; in calling for a discernment of the present needs of the Christian community in faithful continuity with its origins, the Pope encouraged the development of new forms of ministry for a renewed pastoral activity. "Such ministries, apparently new but closely tied up with the Church's living experience down the centuries, such as that of catechists... are valuable for the establishment, life, and growth of the Church, and for her capacity to influence her surroundings and to reach those who are remote from her" (SAINT PAUL VI, Apostolic Exhortation *Evangelii Nuntiandi*, 73).

To be sure, "there has been a growing awareness of the identity and mission of the laity in the Church. We can indeed count on many lay persons, although still not nearly enough, who have a deeply-rooted sense of community and great fidelity to the tasks of charity, catechesis and the celebration of the faith" (*Evangelii Gaudium*, 102). It follows that the reception of a lay ministry such as that of Catechist will emphasize even more the missionary commitment proper to every baptized person, a commitment that must however be carried out in a fully "secular" manner, avoiding any form of clericalization.

8. This ministry has a definite vocational aspect, as evidenced by the Rite of Institution, and consequently calls for due discernment on the part of the Bishop. It is in fact a stable form of service rendered to the local Church in accordance with pastoral needs identified by the local Ordinary, yet one carried out as a work of the laity, as demanded by the very nature of the ministry. It is fitting that those called to the instituted ministry of Catechist be men and women of deep faith and human maturity, active participants in the life of the Christian community, capable of welcoming others, being generous and living a life of fraternal communion. They should also receive suitable biblical, theological, pastoral and pedagogical formation to be competent communicators of the truth of the

faith and they should have some prior experience of catechesis (cf. SECOND VATICAN ECUMENICAL COUNCIL, Decree on the Pastoral Office of Bishops in the Church *Christus Dominus*, 14; CIC can. 231 §1; CCEO can. 409 §1). It is essential that they be faithful co-workers with priests and deacons, prepared to exercise their ministry wherever it may prove necessary, and motivated by true apostolic enthusiasm.

Therefore, after having taken all things into consideration, and by apostolic authority

I establish
the lay ministry of Catechist

The Congregation for Divine Worship and the Discipline of the Sacraments will soon publish the Rite of Institution of the lay ministry of Catechist.

9. I invite the Episcopal Conferences to render effective the ministry of Catechist, determining the necessary process of formation and the normative criteria for admission to this ministry and devising the most appropriate forms for the service which these men and women will be called to exercise in

conformity with the content of this Apostolic Letter.

10.The Synods of the Oriental Churches or the Assemblies of Hierarchs may adopt what is established here for their respective Churches *sui iuris*, in accordance with their particular law.

11.Bishops should make every effort to comply with the exhortation of the Council Fathers: "Pastors… know that they were not established by Christ to undertake by themselves the entire saving mission of the Church to the world. They appreciate, rather, that it is their exalted task to shepherd the faithful and at the same time acknowledge their ministries and charisms so that all in their separate ways, but of one mind, may cooperate in the common task" (*Lumen Gentium*, 30). May the discernment of the gifts that the Holy Spirit never fails to grant to the Church sustain their efforts to make the lay ministry of Catechist effective for the growth of their communities.

I order that what has been laid down by this Apostolic Letter issued "Motu Proprio" have firm and stable effect, anything to the contrary notwithstanding, even if worthy of special mention, and that it be promulgated by publication in *L'Osservatore Romano*, taking effect that same day, and published thereafter in the official commentary of the *Acta Apostolicae Sedis*.

Given in Rome, at Saint John Lateran, on the tenth day of May in the year 2021, the liturgical memorial of Saint John of Avila, Priest and Doctor of the Church, the ninth of my Pontificate.

Franciscus

www.ingramcontent.com/pod-product-compliance
Ingram Content Group UK Ltd.
Pitfield, Milton Keynes, MK11 3LW, UK
UKHW021643190726
13853UKWH00001B/18

9 788826 606293